My First
Alphabet
Dot-to-Dot

Illustrated by Jake McDonald
Written by Elizabeth Golding
Designed by Becca Wildman

B.E.S.
PUBLISHING

First edition for North America published
in 2019 by B.E.S. Publishing Co.

Copyright © iSeek Ltd. 2018

All inquiries should be addressed to:
B.E.S. Publishing Co.
250 Wireless Boulevard
Hauppauge, New York 11788
www.bes-publishing.com

This book was conceived, created, and
produced by iSeek Ltd.
RH17 5PA UK

ISBN: 978-1-4380-1270-4

Date of Manufacture: December 2018

Manufactured by: Shenzhen Caimei Printing Co.,
Shenzhen, China

Printed in China

9 8 7 6 5 4 3 2 1

Go alphadotty!

This book is jam-packed with lots of fun dot-to-dot puzzles, using the letters of the alphabet instead of numbers. Use a pencil, felt-tip pen, or colored pencils to follow the letters in each dot-to-dot. There is a question to answer on each page too!

The puzzles get harder as you turn each page. Don't worry if you get stuck with anything. The answers are at the back of the book.

The dot-to-dot pictures look good colored in. Choose your favorite colored pencils or felt-tip pens and color in as little or as much as you like.

When do you see me?

You see me at n___t.

How many wheels do I have?

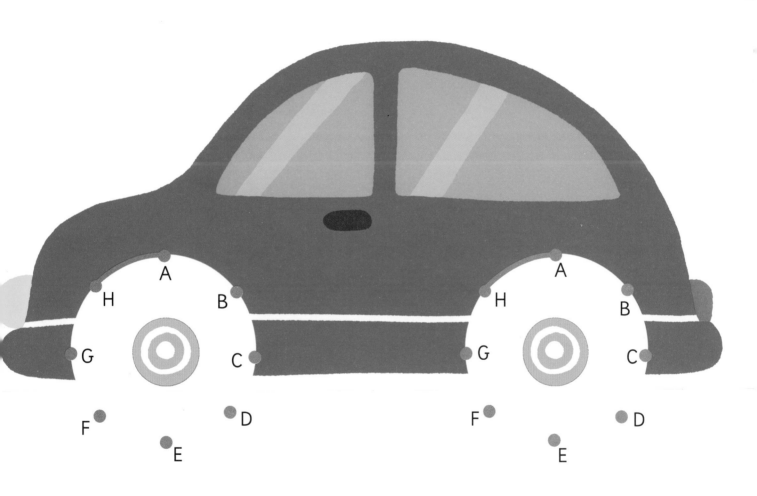

I have ☐ w____s.

How many balloons can you see?

I see ☐ balloons.

Where am I flying?

I am flying in the s___.

What fruits can you see?

I can see an a_ _ _ _e, a p_ _r, and an o_ _ _ _e.

What am I?

I am an a____m c___k.

How many flowers can you see?

I see ⬜ flowers.

What name will you give the teddy?

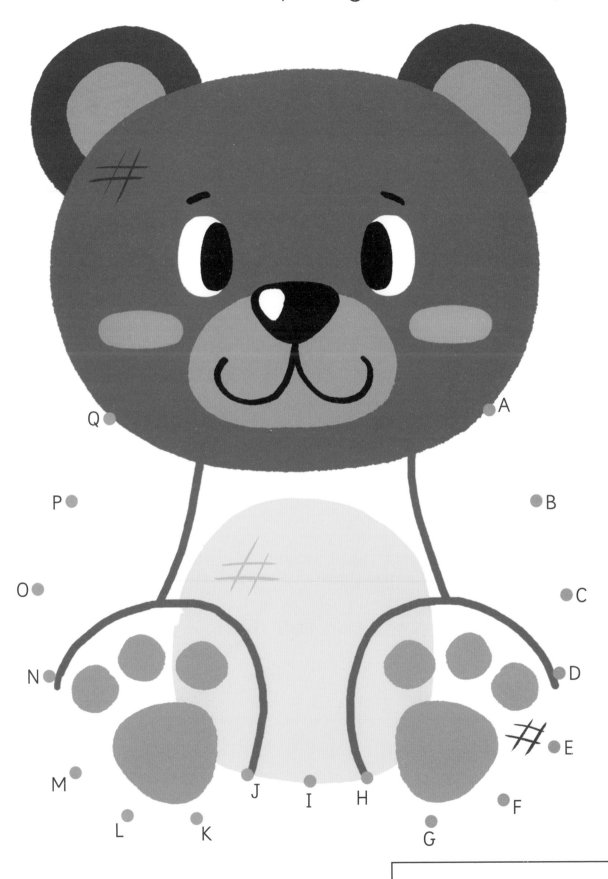

The teddy bear's name is [ ].

What am I?

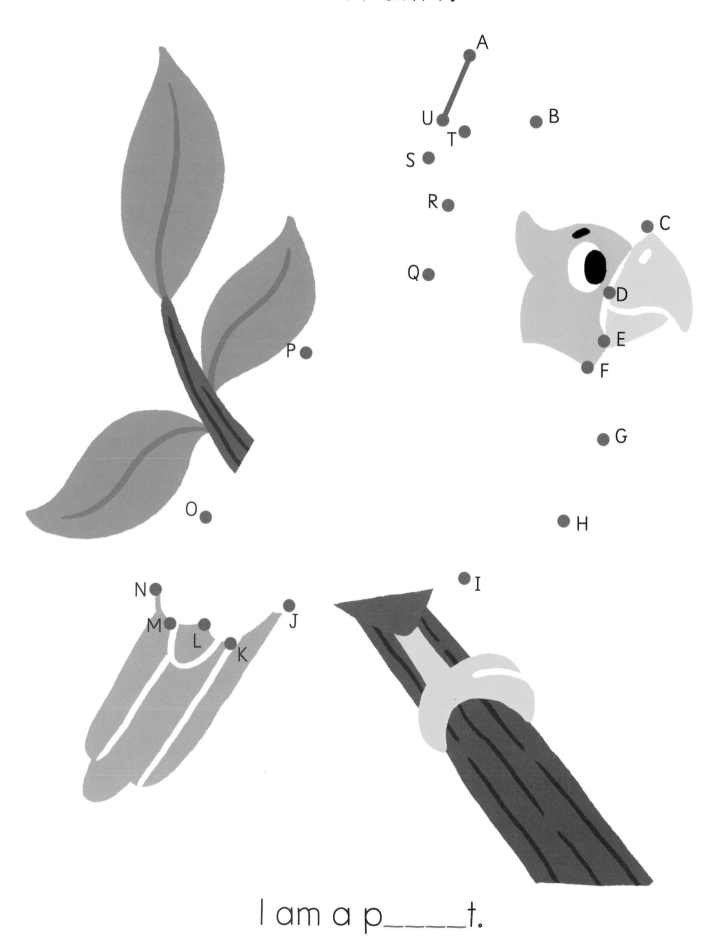

I am a p_____t.

Where do you play with these?

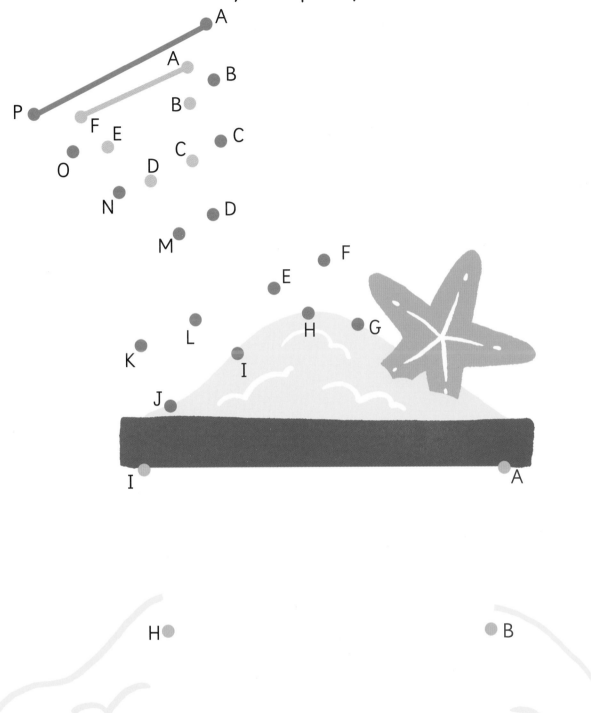

I can play with these at the b___h.

This animal has a shell. What is it?

S
R
T
Q
A
B
C
D
E
P
O
F
N
G
M
H
L
I
K
J

This is a t____e.

Where is this boat sailing?

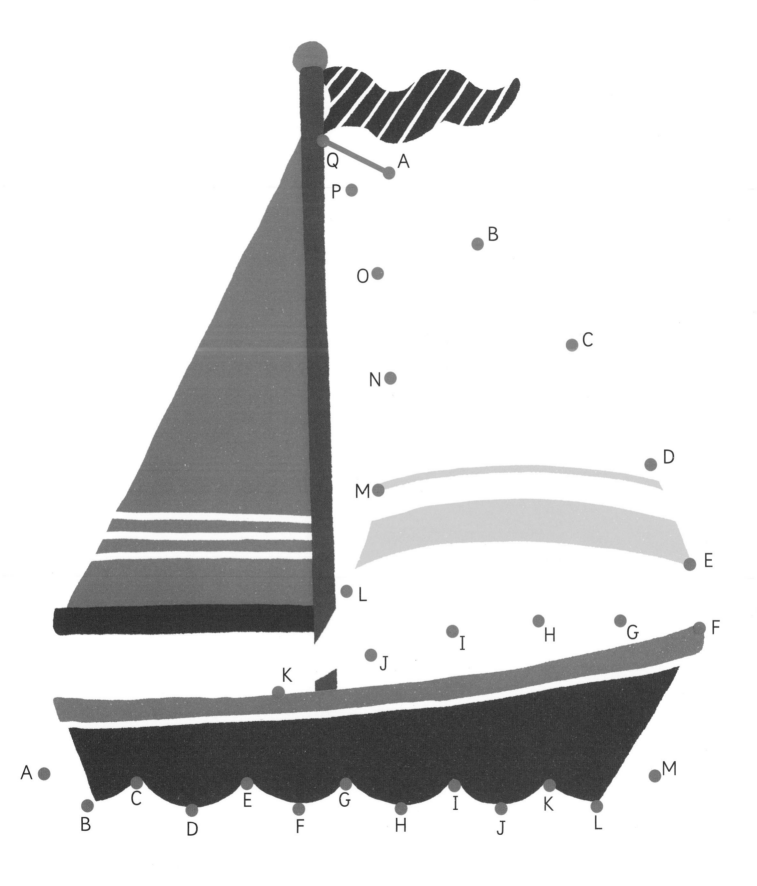

The boat is sailing on the s___.

These are yummy. What are they?

They are c_____s.

What is this?

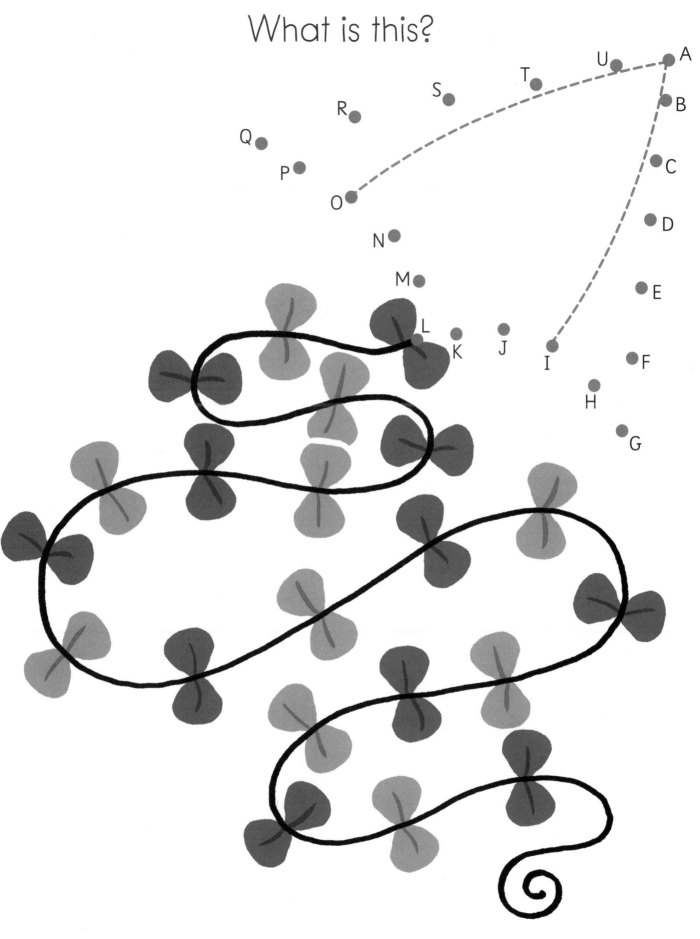

This is a k____.

Who lives here?

A h__ lives here.

What is the puppy looking for?

The puppy is looking for a b____.

How many spots are on this ladybug?

The ladybug has ⬜ spots.

What is the cat driving?

The cat is driving a t_____.

How many stars can you count?

I can count ⬜ stars.

How many balls is the clown juggling?

The clown is juggling ☐ balls.

How many legs does this creature have?

This is an octopus and it has ☐ legs.

What is this?

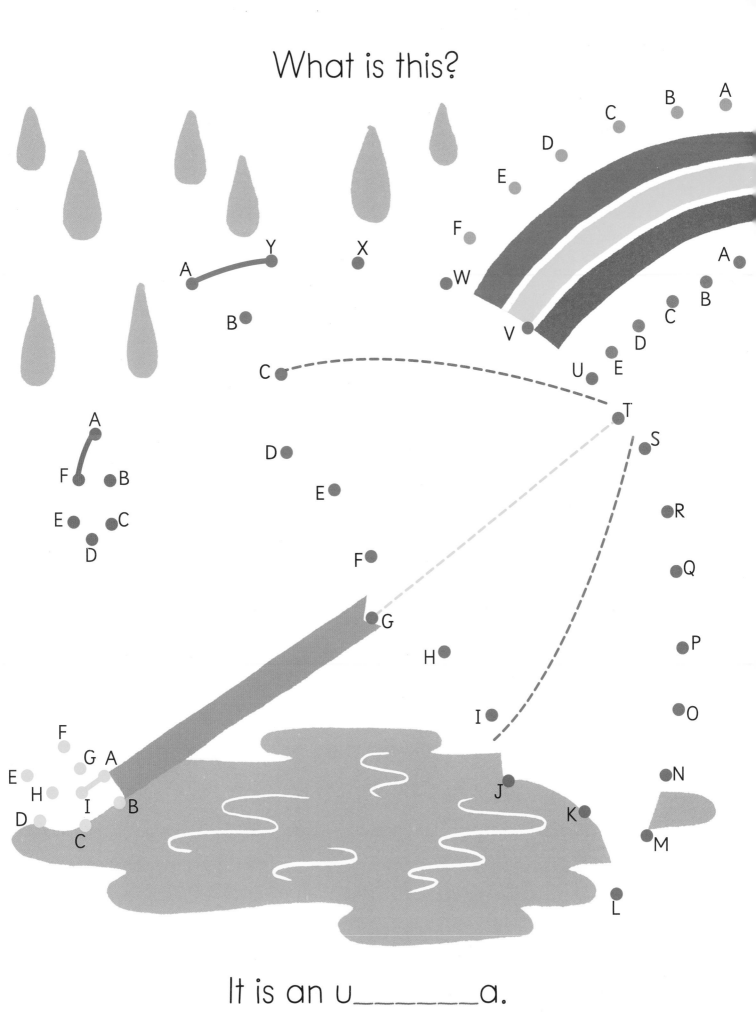

It is an u_____a.

Who is popping out of the box?

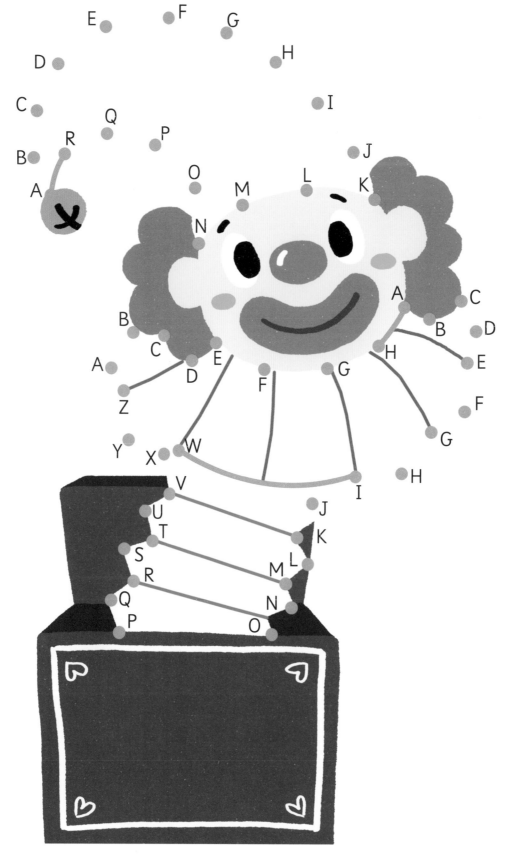

A j__k in a b__ is popping out of the box.

How many hedgehogs can you see?

I can see ☐ hedgehogs.

This looks tasty! What is it?

It is a _____.

What is this insect?

This insect is a b_____y.

What is this panda eating?

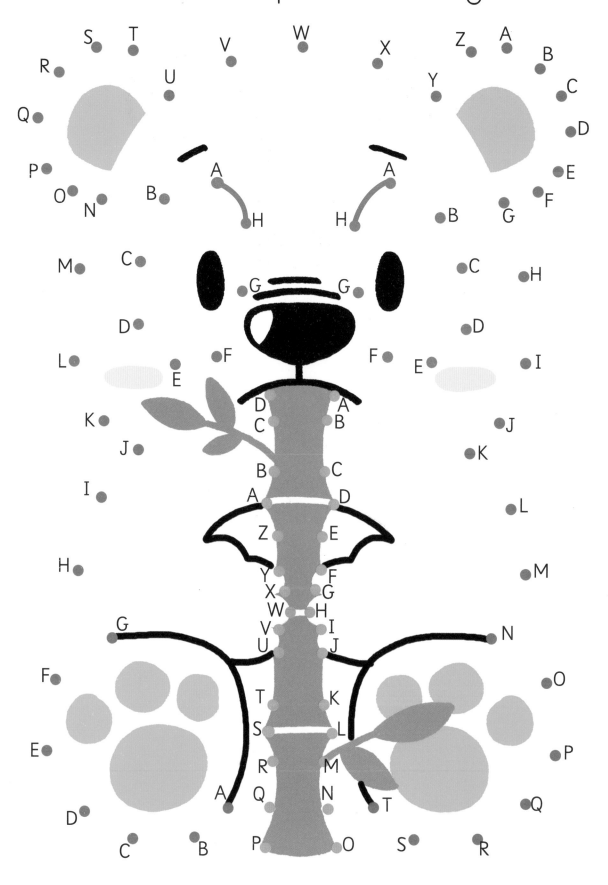

The panda is eating b_____o.

What is this lady doing?

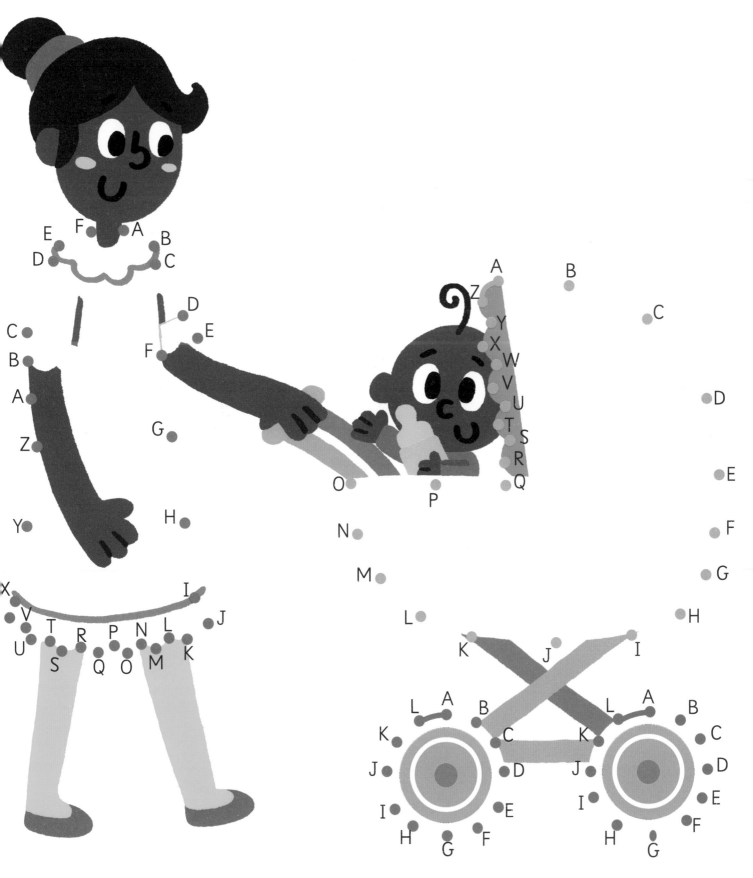

She is p_____g a baby carriage.

How many coins can you see?

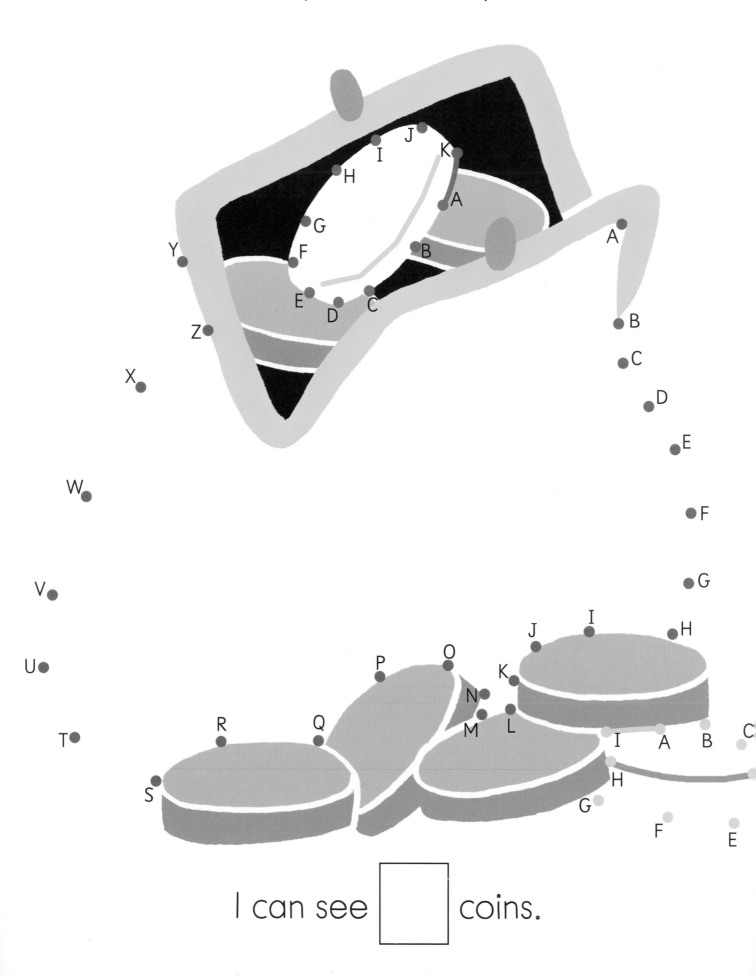

I can see ☐ coins.

How many monkeys are playing?

There are ☐ monkeys.

What is this building called?

It is called a w_____l.

What is this instrument?

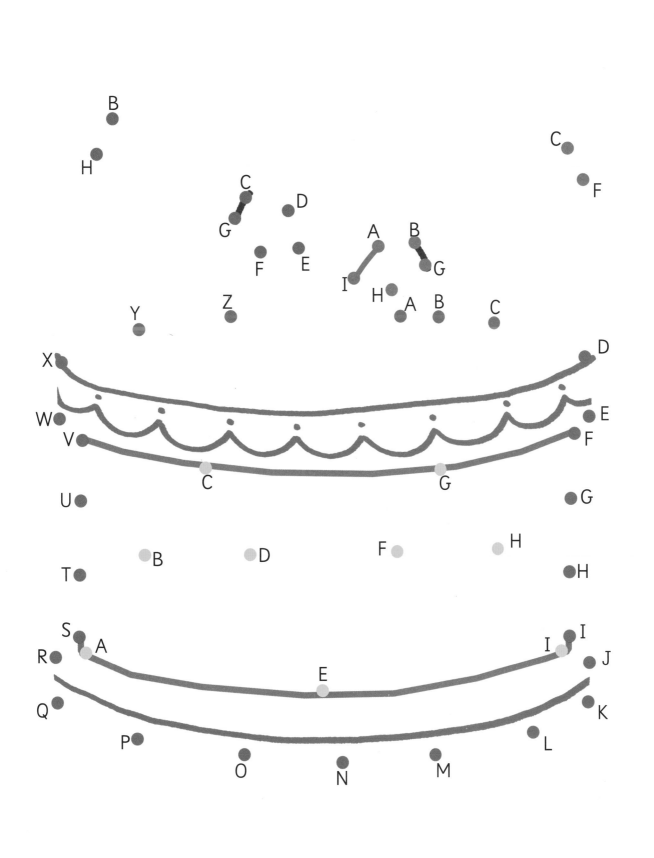

It is a d__m.

What is this animal?

This is a u_____n.

What do bees make?

Bees make h___y.

Where are the animals?

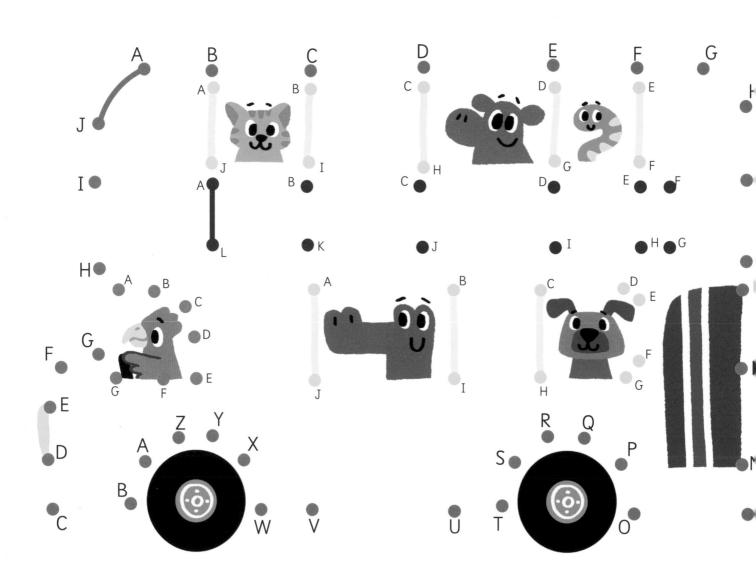

They are on a b_s.

What am I?

I am a r___t.

What is eating the leaves?

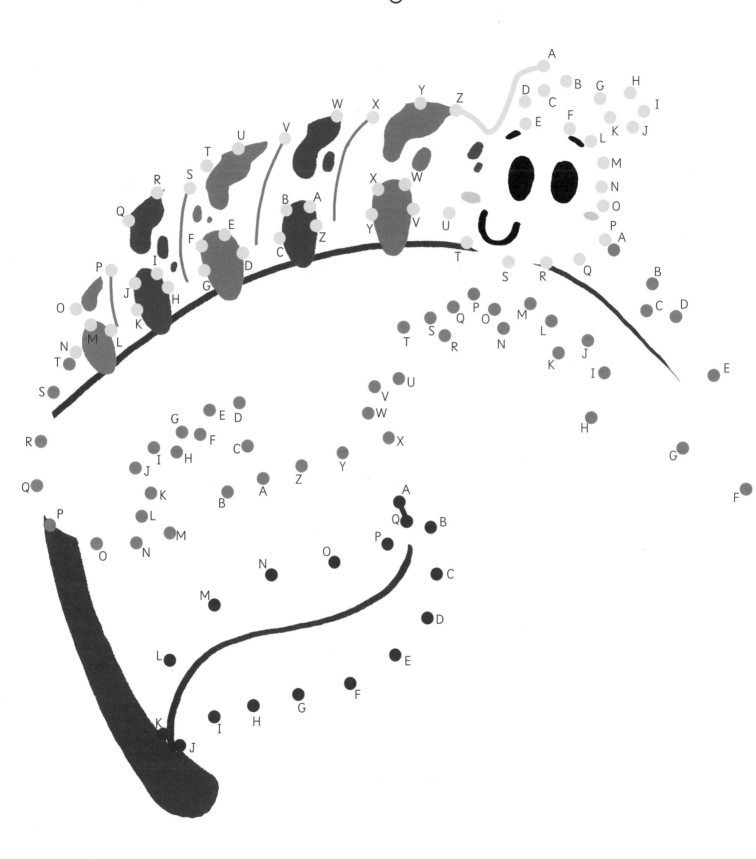

A c_____r is eating the leaves.

Where is this rocket?

The rocket is in s_____.

How many windows can you count?

I can count ☐ windows.

Who is this under the sea?

A m_____d is under the sea.

How many apples can you count?

I can count ☐ apples.

What is the fairy sitting on?

The fairy is sitting on a t_____l.

Who is chasing the mouse?

A c___ is chasing the mouse.

What can you see in the bowl?

I can see a f__h in the bowl.

What game are the children playing?

The children are playing s_____r.

What is on the top of each cupcake?

A c_ _ _ _ y is on top of each cupcake.

What is the pirate holding?

The pirate is holding a s___d.

What are baby frogs called?

Baby frogs are called t_____s.

Make up a funny name for these monsters.

and

Who is the little girl with the three bears?

The little girl is G_____s.

Who frightens the birds away?

A s_____w frightens the birds away.

What are baby ducks called?

Baby ducks are called d_____s.

What are these called?

These creatures are called d_____s.

What is the knight fighting?

He is fighting a d_____n.

How many flying saucers can you count?

I can count ☐ flying saucers.

Where are the children playing?

The children are playing on the b____h.

night

2

3

sky

apple, pear, orange

alarm clock

5

parrot

beach

turtle

sea

cookies

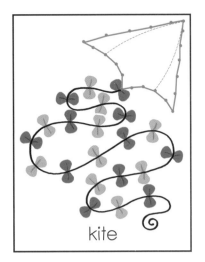

kite

hen

bone

4

train

15

5

8

umbrella

jack in a box

3

cupcake

butterfly

bamboo

pushing

8

3

windmill

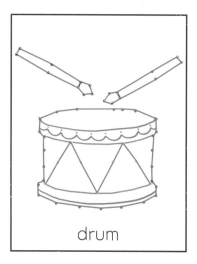

drum

unicorn

honey

bus

robot

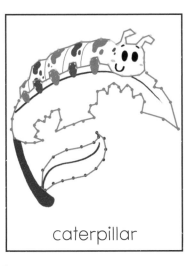

caterpillar

space

3

mermaid

12

toadstool

cat

fish

soccer

cherry

sword

tadpoles

Goldilocks

scarecrow

ducklings

dinosaurs

dragon

3

beach